B R I T A I N   I N   O L D   P

CW00468941

ST IVES BAY
REVISITED

ST IVES TRUST ARCHIVE STUDY CENTRE
AND HAYLE COMMUNITY ARCHIVE

The
History
Press

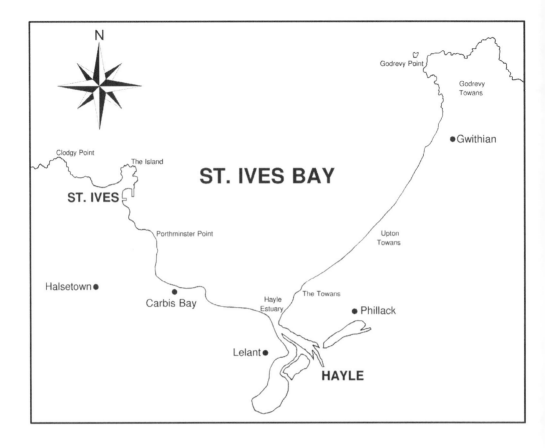

N

Godrevy Point

Godrevy
Towans

●Gwithian

Clodgy Point

The Island

ST. IVES BAY

ST. IVES

Porthminster Point

Upton
Towans

Halsetown ●

Carbis Bay

Hayle
Estuary

The Towans

● Phillack

Lelant ●

HAYLE

First published 2010
Reprinted 2012, 2013

The History Press
The Mill, Brimscombe Port
Stroud, Gloucestershire, GL5 2QG
www.thehistorypress.co.uk

ISBN 978 0 7524 5461 0

Typesetting and origination by The History Press
Printed in Great Britain

CONTENTS

ACKNOWLEDGEMENTS

In addition to the many people who have allowed us to use their images in this book, we would like to thank: Jonathan Holmes; John Allan of the St Ives Photographic Department; Ruth Tonks of the Lelant History Trust; Brian and Margaret Stevens of the St Ives Museum; Mr J. Hornsey, Mrs Doris Clark; Mrs Doris Clark; John Pollard; and Geoff Hichens for the St Ives group photo.

The Hayle Archive members involved with this book – Georgina Schofield, Chris Quick, John Farrar and Pat Millett – would like to thank the following for their help and support: Harveys Foundry Trust; the County Records Office , for access to the Bate Collection; Eileen Williams, wife of the late Ronnie Williams for access to his collection; Trevor and Betty Millett; Eileen Couch; Kenneth Lang; and Winnie Bassett.

Front cover: Ben Phillips with his horse and cart by the gig *Our Boys*, St Ives Harbour, August 1956. (David Elsbury)

INTRODUCTION

In 1995 Jonathan Holmes, Museum Officer at the Penzance and District Museum & Art Gallery (now known as Penlee House Gallery & Museum) assembled a large number of photographs of St Ives and Hayle for the first edition of *St Ives Bay*. This was probably the first time that a wide-ranging book of photographs had been locally sourced from images of the whole area, and Jonathan must be congratulated for putting this together from a number of public and private collections in West Cornwall.

Fourteen years later, the production of *St Ives Bay Revisited* by The History Press is a community initiative. The choice of photographs and their descriptions has been taken over by a team of volunteers from the St Ives Trust Archive Study Centre, which opened in 1996, and by volunteers from the very newly created Hayle Community Archive. Each member of the team has specialist knowledge of a particular aspect of the area.

Both organisations have access to many more photographic images than were publicly available in 1995, and these cover scenes from the earliest days of photography to the present time. Thanks to the Heritage Lottery Fund, the Archive Study Centre has been able to digitize and catalogue its extensive collection. Opportunities for understanding and researching local history have grown enormously in recent years. Community archives are bringing to both residents and visitors alike an awareness of their culture which is making historians of us all. Everyone has a story to tell and images of the place in which they live to share with others.

St Ives Bay is rich in history. Despite its small geographical area, the individual towns contained within its boundaries are varied, yet each in their own way has played a vital role, both economically and culturally, in many parts of the world. At the same time, its distance from all the main cities in the United Kingdom gives it a remoteness which has proven to be both a disadvantage and a benefit.

The compilers have divided St Ives Bay into individual areas, and within each have covered its diversity. It is therefore possible to look at St Ives and Hayle through such headings as businesses and shops, religion, education, local characters, events, ceremonies, customs, the harbour, fishing, wreck and rescue, art, trades, mining, transport and tourism. The smaller communities of Carbis Bay, Lelant and Halsetown are treated as individual locations.

St Ives as a town only really began to expand at the beginning of the nineteenth century, although the fine Parish Church was built 400 years earlier. A small fishing community, almost cut off from the rest of Cornwall by land, but with excellent sea connections, was nevertheless granted a Charter by King Charles I to become a Borough in 1639. For many years it was known for being a 'rotten borough' in parliamentary terms as, despite its small population and almost complete absence of a middle or professional class, St Ives continued to send two Members of Parliament to Westminster until the Reform Act of 1832.

St Ives has a proud maritime history. Its seine fisheries sent off shiploads of pilchards to Italy from Tudor times. Much of the geography of Downlong, the old fishing quarter, is still based on the former fish cellars which were used to salt and press the pilchards. Each spring saw the mackerel boats fit out for the deep water fishery in the Celtic Sea and west of the Isles of Scilly.

St Ives' boats fished the Irish herring from 1816-1961 and its boatbuilders built sturdy Cornish luggers for Ireland, the Isle of Man and the west of Scotland. By the mid-nineteenth century they joined the North Sea herring fishery. Each September the Cornish boats raced each other down the North Sea and through the Channel, bringing presents of Scarborough rock and Whitby jet for their families at home.

October brought the herring to St Ives Bay and the boatyards rang with the sounds of planes and caulking mallets as new herring gigs were built. A friendly haze over the smoke houses showed where the kipper girls were hard at work. Fish are still landed in St Ives. Our little mackerel punts are renowned for top-quality catches, but they are only a fraction of former times.

Cornish tin and copper were essential elements of the Bronze Age. But this early mineral exploration was not mining in the modern sense. Alluvial tin deposits were worked for centuries, and tin 'streaming', as it was called, lasted in some parts of Cornwall well into the twentieth century. The Stennack, St Ives' central road, takes its name from two Cornish words *sten* and *ack*, meaning 'tin place'. Tin working around the Stennack stream lasted for generations. During the eighteenth and nineteenth centuries, deep mining developed along the lodes running under the town from Rosewall and Ransome United, on Rosewall Hill, and down to St Ives Consols in the upper Stennack, then to Trenwith and North Providence right on the water's edge at Pednolver Point. Many local places still retain their mining names; for example, Parc an Stamps, where the ore was once crushed; Wheal Venture; Wheal Speed and Wheal Margery at Carbis Bay and Pannier Lane where, long ago, lines of patient mules carried away their baskets of copper ore.

Hayle, a bustling mining port, developed into a busy foundry town around its two rival works, Harvey's and the Cornish Copper Co., which supplied the latest Cornish pumping engines to mines as far away as Mexico and Peru. It too had its neighbouring mines, most notably Wheal Alfred.

By the 1870s the price of Cornish tin plummeted, the result of cheaper alluvial deposits in Malaysia and Australia. The Cornish diaspora, already begun, accelerated as a result of the failure of the local mines and the 'Cousin Jacks', as the miners were called, took their hard-rock mining skills around the world.

The personalities and characters of St Ives are many and diverse, from fishwives to poets, sportsmen and ship owners. In a book such as this we can only show a few of the sons and daughters of the town.

The culture of St Ives Bay shares much with that of Cornwall, but has some distinct traditions. Here we have a snapshot of our customs, some long extinct, some flourishing and, happily, some comparatively recently revived. A number of our Celtic-derived traditions were dying out in the early twentieth century, but have more recently increased in popularity.

The very nature of the Cornish coast with its rugged cliffs, combined with high winds and powerful storms, means that from time to time ships will meet their end, either on the rocks or some sandy shore. The Royal National Lifeboat Institution, which first established a station in St Ives in 1860, has provided the town with a succession of lifeboats down the years. It has been instrumental in helping to save the lives of many shipwrecked sailors. A major disaster took place on 23 January 1939 when the *John and Sarah Eliza Stych* capsized, and seven men out of her crew of eight were drowned in heavy seas in St Ives Bay.

Christian tradition has had an important role since, according to legend, St Eia arrived from Ireland, sailing on a leaf in the fifth century. Lelant and Carbis Bay's two saints, Uny and Anta, came by more conventional means. Lelant was the mother church of the area until St Ives completed its own fine Parish Church in 1426.

Charles and John Wesley's mission in the mid-eighteenth century revolutionised the religious life of the district, which still retains a strong Methodist identity. Alcohol created many social problems in eighteenth- and nineteenth-century Cornwall, leading to a lively Temperance movement which included the Band of Hope, Teetotal Methodists and Rechabites, who encouraged members to sign the pledge to refrain from drinking alcohol.

Dames' schools provided a rudimentary education service which often amounted to little more than child minding. Since the 1600s there were also many private ventures. Captain Short's Navigation School on Barnoon Hill served generations of St Ives' mariners. Lelant National (Church) School was one of the earliest in the district followed by St Ives National School, opened in 1847 opposite the Parish Church (and currently the home of the St Ives Trust Archive Study Centre). The Sunday schools and Methodist schools made valiant efforts. The opening of Board Schools at St Ives and Trevarrack, near Lelant, and the introduction of compulsory elementary education soon afterwards, greatly widened educational opportunities. St Ives 1881 Board School still has an important function in the community as the Stennack Surgery.

It was the advent of the branch railway line in 1877, from what is now known as St Erth, which transformed the life of the town. Over the previous twenty years the decline in the mining industry had decimated the local population, which reached a low of about 6,000 inhabitants. However, a professional class began to emerge in the middle of the nineteenth century and rows of Victorian terraces and villas were built on the hills around the harbour, away from the continual smell of the fish. The railway brought many visitors to the town, which led to the construction of hotels and the conversion of larger houses into small hotels and guesthouses.

As the popularity of St Ives increased, even the people living in cottages in the Downlong area, around the harbour, offered bed and breakfast during the summer holidays. The roads became busier as more visitors came in by car and, consequently, buildings had to be demolished to widen roads and make space for car parking. Fortunately most of the original narrow streets in this area still remain, but sadly many of the cottages are no longer family homes. They have become 'holiday lets' and the sight of washing lines across the streets is a thing of the past. The increase in the 'Uplong' population in the upper parts of the town led to the need for more shops and services, providing everything for everyday living. Prior to this there would only have been the small shops in Downlong, most of which were rooms in people's houses.

The modern visitor to St Ives has the choice of four beach locations (including the harbour), each very different in character. All of the beaches have played a part in the fishing industry and have undergone a gradual transformation as tourism has evolved.

As well as tourism, St Ives is probably best-known for the artists who have lived and worked in the town since the 1880s. The clean air and extraordinary light encouraged painters from around the world who were developing the techniques of working outdoors to come to the far south-west of the country by train. When they arrived, they found a picturesque landscape and townscape and, more importantly, large north-facing lofts situated around the beaches, now lying empty because of the gradual demise of the fishing industry. Soon art schools, art organisations, picture framers and galleries began to appear, and painters could be seen on every street corner. At the beginning of the Second World War and during the next decade, a new wave of artists arrived in the town. This group of Modernists was led by painter Ben Nicholson and sculptor Barbara Hepworth, and in the late 1940s and '50s St Ives was pre-eminent in avant-garde art, equal only to the work of the Abstract Expressionists being promoted in New York. It was to celebrate the work of these artists, as well as the legacy of the world-famous potter Bernard Leach, who arrived in St Ives in 1920, that Tate St Ives was opened in 1993, reversing the trend towards foreign holidays.

Halsetown is named after James Halse, a solicitor who was born in Truro. He wished to become a Member of Parliament for St Ives, and because he was involved in the St Ives Consols Mines, he decided to build about eighty granite cottages for his growing workforce of miners in exchange for their votes. Each house had its own small plot of land and, along with the inn, the cottages were laid out on a garden city plan. The village has now become a desirable residential area, enjoying conservation and Heritage status. In 1876 the population was recorded as 1,810, whilst today it has a mere 154 names on the electoral register. Halsetown's Parish Church, situated on the outskirts of St Ives, actually lies about 1½ miles from Halsetown village.

The area now known as Carbis Bay was originally a collection of small hamlets and farms, such as Chyangweal, Higher Carbence and Boskerris Wartha. The place name did not exist until the Great Western Railway built the branch line and called the station Carbis Bay. Amongst the farms there were engine houses and other buildings associated with the mining industry. In the nineteenth century, the Wheal Providence Mine, producing both tin and copper, employed hundreds of people. After the collapse of the mining industry, the engine houses were demolished and the mountains of waste were used to fill the shafts. Porthrepta Beach has become a popular attraction for holidaymakers, evolving from the days when, with its adjacent tea gardens, it was a popular destination for Sunday school 'tea treats'. Extensive housing developments have gradually transformed the area, spreading over the fields surrounding Carbis Valley, up onto the moorland and northwards to merge with St Ives.

If you drive through Lelant today, you will find an attractive, prosperous-looking village with a lot of new housing and a growing population. But, despite these appearances, Lelant has coped with several changes which have threatened its way of life during its long history; firstly, the rise in importance of St Ives and, secondly, the influx of sand that silted the channel and rendered the harbour unworkable. From the sixteenth century, the centre of population was forced to migrate further south along the estuary and up to higher ground inland. Thirdly, the running down of the tin and copper mines caused considerable unemployment. Today the threat to the village is dwindling services and amenities. A century ago Lelant was practically self-supporting and boasted about forty businesses and services. Today these have been reduced to a mere handful. But, in fact, Lelant's story goes back to long before history was written down, and is far older than St Ives. The present Church of St Uny partly dates back to the late eleventh or early twelfth century, and the parish of Lelant included St Ives, Towednack and Zennor, showing that Lelant was the most important settlement on the north coast of the Penwith peninsula.

Hayle (*Heyl* in Cornish) means estuary, and the estuary from which the town takes its name is one of the few natural harbours on the north Cornish coast. It was an important centre for trade for over 6,000 years; ships from the Mediterranean came seeking tin and copper, bringing with them the early green shoots of Christianity. Trade and religious influence continued to grow, bringing prosperity to the small settlements surrounding the estuary. The later medieval period saw a rapid decline due to silting from the metal extraction along the feeder-rivers. As the eighteenth century dawned, the birth of the Industrial Revolution heralded the growth of Hayle as an urban centre. By 1740, quays were being extended to facilitate the import of coal and other goods, as mining and metal smelting increased from 1758 onwards.

In 1779 John Harvey established his foundry, and rivalry between the Cornish Copper Co. of Copperhouse and Harvey's Foundry was very bitter. By 1819 the production of pumping engines by both companies brought about closer ties between them. They jointly undertook a major project to build the three largest pumping engines in the world to drain the marshes of Holland. The boom years lasted from 1830 to 1880 and then, as the mines closed down and new developments began to make the great steam engines redundant, Hayle's industry declined and its skilled workforce sought employment outside Cornwall.

In recent years, the harbour has again silted up and shipping and imported goods have ceased. Tourism has replaced commerce and industry. The harbour has changed hands several times and is now poised to undergo major regeneration.

St Ives Bay Revisited tells the story of these lively communities – the tin miners, fishermen, herring girls, sailors, lifeboat men, the artists and tradesmen and their beliefs, enthusiasms,disasters and relaxations in this corner of Cornwall which still retains its strong sense of identity.

1

ST IVES – THE TOWN

General view of St Ives, *c.* 1905. The headland known as the Island forms the backdrop to the town. On the left there is a rocky outcrop, which until 1904 had been the site of the medieval St Nicholas' Chapel (later rebuilt). At the other end of the ridge are the remains of a gun battery which had been dismantled in 1895. The harbour is surrounded by an interesting assortment of buildings in the part of town known as Downlong – the area in the foreground being part of Uplong. Near the Parish Church is the West Pier (built in 1894) on which is a crane used to load ships with stone quarried from Carthew, beyond Porthmeor. This picture was taken soon after the Mariner's Chapel was built (large building on the left, now an art gallery). (Tim & Rita Lait Postcard Collection)

Tregenna Place, 1880s. At that time it was essentially a residential part of the town, but there were a few shops and the Commercial Hotel. On the right is the garden wall of the Manor House, home of the Stephens family before Tregenna Castle was built in 1774. The house remained part of the estate until 1871 and in the 1890s the steamship company of Edward Hain & Son had an office in the building. The Manor House was replaced by a Post Office in 1906 (Tim & Rita Lait Postcard Collection).

Tregenna Place, *c.* 1950. In contrast with the previous picture, this photograph shows a wide range of shops providing people with their everyday needs. For example, on the left is a dairy, Quick's greengrocers, Boots chemists and Liptons grocers. The street is busy with people but there are only a few vehicles, unlike nowadays.

High Street, *c.* 1900. Well-dressed Edwardian ladies walk past the mounting steps outside the Queen's Hotel. The steps have long gone but the frontage remains virtually unchanged, unlike the old building opposite which had been part of the hotel stables. It was demolished and replaced by the Scala cinema which opened in 1920. Despite the fact that this was converted to Boots chemists shop in 1978, the overall façade was retained. (Tim & Rita Lait Postcard Collection)

Lanhams, 1940s. James Kempthorne Lanham opened a shop in the High Street in 1869, listed as a 'fancy repository & tobacconist' in an 1873 directory. He was reputedly encouraged by Whistler to stock artists' materials and in 1887 he opened a gallery over the shop. By 1889 James Lanham's business had diversified, being described as an 'artists' colourman, china, glass & earthenware dealer, general ironmonger & cutler, general draper & furniture dealer, & ale & porter bottler, wine & spirits merchant'. He sold the business in 1912 but it retained his name and the gallery continued to stage exhibitions of artists such as Julius Olsson and S.J. Lamorna Birch. As this picture shows, Lanhams became involved in the property market. Although the broad-based business no longer exists, the company is still in property management, in part of the original High Street shop. (St Ives Archive)

Opposite: Fore Street, 1913. This narrow street was, and still is, very different in character to the High Street. The first shop on the right is that of James Uren White, printer and stationer, who produced the town's first newspaper, the *St Ives Weekly Summary*, first issue dated 25 May 1889. Fore Street shops have gradually changed to attract the visitors and this is currently one of several jewellers. (Tim & Rita Lait Postcard Collection)

Note what FAULL is doing !

He is selling this

MANGLING

and

WRINGING

MACHINE

For **1/-**

(Per week).

Special Discount for Cash.

This Wringer is one of the best, with good hard sycamore Rollers, guaranteed to wear and give satisfaction.

WILLIAM FAULL,
Ironmonger,
(Opposite Post Office)
ST. IVES.

Faull's ironmongers shop, early 1900s. This business in Fore Street was started by Henry Faull in the 1850s, passing through the family to his son, William, and then to grandson Frank Faull. (Confusingly the shop was often shown as No. 5 Fore Street but the modern address is No. 8.) The fact that the 'mangling and wringing machine' is advertised for 1s per week, but does not give the actual price, shows that few people could afford to buy such things outright. (Photograph, above, courtesy of the Paul Martin Collection. Poster, left, courtesy of St Ives Archive)

Jacobs printing works and shop. This business, run by William Johns Jacobs and his brother, James Luke Jacobs, was at No. 15 Fore Street. On 2 September 1899, William printed the first issue of a weekly newspaper, the *Western Echo*, editing it until 1954. A regular item was the tide table, which was invaluable for the Downlong fishing community. The paper merged with the *St Ives Times* in 1957, becoming the *St Ives Times & Echo*. The shop was often advertised in guidebooks – in 1935 it was described as 'one of the most interesting shops in St Ives'. Although the shop front has altered over the years, the arched upper windows remain. (St Ives Archive – late Peter Murrish Collection)

Back Road East, *c.* 1900. This is one of the wider streets in Downlong, with characteristic houses in which the ground floor was used for storage of fishing equipment and the living accommodation was on the first floor, accessed by the external steps. In this picture a fisherman's wife is standing near a communal tap and on the other side of the street is a group of children, most of whom are barefoot. (Tim & Rita Lait Postcard Collection)

Norway, 1890s. A washday scene showing a woman working in her 'wash troy' which is balanced on the wall. Clothing has been laid out to dry on the roof of the adjacent building (demolished in the early 1900s) and there is a washing line near a house in the background. On Mondays there were washing lines on the harbour foreshore, across the streets in Downlong and sheets were laid out to dry on the Island. (Tim & Rita Lait Valentine Postcard Collection)

Bailey's Lane, 1890s. A picture of Downlong people, all wearing hats of differing styles. Originally called Street-Petite, this very narrow lane managed to avoid the 'slum clearance' of the 1930s which resulted in the demolition of many old buildings in the vicinity. (Tim & Rita Lait Postcard Collection)

Virgin Street, *c*. 1900. A pedlar is trying to sell his wares to two women standing in the doorway of their cottage. Various other travelling salesmen, including French onion sellers, regularly visited the town. The very tall chimneys, characteristic of cottages in Downlong, were built using bricks brought in by sea and can be seen in other pictures. (Paul Martin Collection)

The wharf, *c.* 1900. This area near the slipway has changed considerably since the time of this picture, with the construction of Wharf Road and the demolition or modernisation of most of these buildings. Outside Kemp's barbers shop three men are sitting on Doble's Wall, the subject of a song by local poet and bard John Barber. Only part of the wall now remains, in front of the cottage which became the famous Hart's Ice Cream Parlour (closed in 1983). (Tim & Rita Lait Postcard Collection)

White Hart Hotel, *c.* 1910. Originally a plain-fronted building on the wharf, it had been transformed by the addition of the ornate façade. Part of it was the White Hart Stores, James Laity's grocery shop, which specialised in blends of tea. (Older brother William also had a grocery business on the wharf, nearer to Smeaton's Pier.) The building is now completely unrecognisable compared with this picture, but there are a few vestiges of the old stonework. (Tim & Rita Lait Postcard Collection)

2

ST IVES – MARITIME

The most ancient fishing season was pilchard seining. Porthminster Beach was crowded with seine boats, waiting for the pilchards. Here they are lined up under the new Porthminster Hotel, opened in 1894. (John McWilliams Frith Postcard Collection)

In early September, the seiners were 'put into pay'. They loaded their giant nets into the seine boat and anchored off Porthminster Beach, sheltered under their canvas 'tilt'. Pleasure yachts wait for their freight of trippers. (John McWilliams Postcard Collection)

The 'huer' searched the sea for signs of the pilchards from his lookout. When they arrived, his cry of 'Hevva!' brought everyone running. Here he directs the seine boat to shoot its net in a circle round the shoal. His signals were called 'bushes'. (St Ives Museum)

When the fish were enclosed, the 'blowsers' manned their capstans and hauled the net closer to the shore. This was to prevent the fish escaping under the net. (Paul Martin Collection)

Next the 'tuck net' was shot inside the seine and lifted to the surface where a mass of splashing pilchards appeared. The net was surrounded by boats called 'dippers'. Pairs of fishermen dipped their baskets into the wriggling mass and loaded their boats. (St Ives Museum)

The pilchards were taken to the cellars, tipped into tanks and mixed with salt. Next they were pressed to expel the train oil. Carefully packed in barrels, they were exported to Italy in sailing ships. Here a group of cellar workers pose for the camera. (Andrew Lanyon)

The mackerel season began in March, forty miles north-west of St Ives. Later the shoals moved westward and the fleet worked from the Isles of Scilly. Here the mackerel boats *Good Templar* SS 516, *Arethusa* SS 439 and *Misty Morn* SS 585 leave harbour on a quiet day. (John McWilliams Postcard Collection)

When the mackerel boats landed their catch, there was no hanging about. Here, the boats are anchored off the harbour. Their small boats, punts, land the catch on the harbour sand. On the right a lugger is off to sea again. They hope to reach the fishing grounds by nightfall. (John McWilliams Postcard Collection)

The first Lowestoft boats came to Cornwall in 1860. The deeply devout St Ives fishermen banned those which fished on a Sunday. The first Lowestoft steam drifter was built in 1897. Soon hundreds of East Coast steam drifters came to the Cornish mackerel season. In March 1907, the steam drifter *Result* LT 259, anchored on the left, landed 3,500 mackerel at St Ives which sold for 15-16s per 120 fish. (Royal Cornwall Museum, Truro)

Above: By 1911 the steam drifters from Lowestoft and Yarmouth had made the St Ives mackerel luggers out of date. The steam boats could go to sea when the luggers were becalmed or weather-bound. The beautiful St Ives luggers were laid up in a row along the estuary at Lelant 'to die', as the fishermen said. Fourteen were sold to Irish fishing ports, mainly Kilkeel, at rock bottom prices between £100 and £150. Their fishermen emigrated to the USA or signed on in the local Hain Shipping Line. (Tim & Rita Lait Postcard Collection)

Left: When the mackerel season finished in June, the boats put in herring nets to fish in Ireland and the North Sea. Here the crew of the *Endeavour* SS 568, the youngest to sail north, pose for the camera. From left to right, back row: Dan Quick, Joe Murrish, James H. Quick, W. Cocking. Front row: Edwin Bottrell, James Cocking, Dick Mills Care. Each September, St Ives children looked forward to their dads' return with presents of Scarborough rock. (Private Collection)

The *Jane* left St Ives for the North Sea herring fishery on 10 July 1895. She fished from Berwick, North Sunderland and Scarborough and arrived home on 20 September, having earned £110 3*d* for twenty-six nights' work. Each of her crew earned £5 18*s* 3*d*. (Margaret Stratton)

In June the boats sailed to the Irish herring season at Arklow, Wicklow, Howth, Kingstown (Dun Laughaire), Kilkeel and Ardglass, where in 1876 there were 140 Scots, twenty Manx, forty-two Irish and nineteen Cornish boats. Here the St Ives lugger *Margaret* SS 47 is moored at Ardglass. The first St Ives boat fished the Irish herring in 1816. (Michael Craine)

Here the *Sweet Promise*, temporarily registered in Waterford, loads a ring net to sail to Dunmore East in Ireland in December 1960. Her skipper, Ernest Stevens Junior, was a talented fisherman. This was the last St Ives voyage to fish the Irish herring. (Francis McWilliams)

From the 1890s the St Ives herring season thrived. The season began in October and lasted until after Christmas. In this scene from the 1920s the boats are going to sea. (John McWilliams Postcard Collection)

This gig's crew are hard at work unmeshing herring from their nets. The inflated 'buffs' or 'mollacs', which kept the nets afloat, are piled around her lantern. SS 148 is the *Thrive*. (Private Collection)

The herring were carried up from the beach in two-handled boxes called 'gurries', which contained about twenty-eight stones of fish. In the background is the well-known steam boat *Pioneer* PZ 277. Restored by Jim Richards, the *Pioneer* still sails from Hayle. (John McWilliams Postcard Collection)

All around the harbour the herring were counted from the gurries into barrels by women. 120 fish made a long hundred. Two women stood at the end of each gurry and counted out loud. When they got to 120, they called out 'Score Ma!' and the skipper's wife made a tally mark in her notebook. Here, carts are being loaded with barrels of herring destined for the kipper houses or the railway station. (Private Collection)

St Ives' kipper houses were Rouncefield's on the Prom, Pawlyn's in Fish Street, Holmes' in Fish Street, Brown's at the Rope Walk, Veal's by the Island Meadow and Woodger's at Porthgwidden. In this photo, kipper girls are hard at work at Woodger's under gas light. (St Ives Archive – William Thomas Collection)

From 1919-1947, nearly forty shallow draft motor gigs were built, mainly to fish the herring, by Tommy Thomas on the Prom, Lander in Back Road East and Henry Trevorrow on Harbour Beach. Here the boatbuilder has a critical audience. (John McWilliams Postcard Collection)

A small crowd watches a gig being launched from the Wharf on a high spring tide. St Ives' first motor gig, the *Glorious Peace* SS 37, was launched in 1919. This could be her. At this time the Wharf Road had yet to be completed. It was finished in 1922. (*St Ives Times & Echo*)

Until the 1960s, St Ives' boats fished the summer pilchard season from Newlyn. This was called 'Going to the Wolf', because they often fished around the Wolf Rock Lighthouse. In this 1950s scene, the crews of the *Freeman* SS 65, *Sweet Promise* SS 95 and *Sea Cormorant* SS 155 yarn in the sun. Recently, Cornish pilchards have been re-branded Cornish sardines. (St Ives Archive)

Mackerel, herring and pilchards were caught at night with fragile cotton drift nets which had to be carefully looked after. They were barked in a hot cutch liquid to preserve them (cutch bark came from Borneo). Here Skipper John F. Toman of the *Nazarene* SS 114 and his crew spread their nets on the Island to dry. (St Ives Archive)

Left: White fish were caught with baited hooks. Here two old fellows bait their lines which they called 'small tayckle' into boxes called 'rips'. They coil their lines into the 'rips' and arrange the baited hooks neatly along the back. When not in use, the hooks were kept tidy in a grooved stick called a 'claw'. (St Ives Museum)

Below: The *Our John* SS 64 was built for the Barber family in 1926. Sadly William and Matthew Barber were lost in the 1939 lifeboat disaster. Here the *Our John* has her deck full of line baskets. Between the two centre fishermen is the line hauler, known as the 'jinny'. (St Ives Archive)

Left: Each summer, the liners worked the shore grounds between St Ives and Lands End. Sand eels were used for bait. Here George Care baits lines aboard the *Lamorna* SS 45. It was fiddly work. (David Elsbury)

Below: The fish were carted to the Slipway, spread out for sale, then cleaned and packed on the fish plats along the Prom. The Food Standards Agency might take a dim view of this 1920s scene. (Private Collection)

In this 1940s scene Smeaton's Pier is full of crab pots waiting to go aboard the row of crabbing gigs, left centre. St Ives crab pots were made to a special design using wire to resist the ground swell on the north Cornish coast. They were shot in 'tiers' of thirty. (John McWilliams Postcard Collection)

St Ives was a fishing port but also handled cargo. In this busy scene, two ketches and three schooners wait to unload into carts. On the left, Mr J.T. Short's ancient schooner *Annie* serves as a Monday clothes prop. (John McWilliams Collection)

Vessels needed a pilot to guide them safely into harbour. Here a pilot gig is rowed away under the bow of a visiting schooner which is taking in her sails. Often several pilot gigs would race out to a vessel. The first pilot to arrive got the job. St Ives Pilot Gig Club operates from Carbis Bay Beach most summer evenings at 6.00 p.m. (St Ives Archive)

The ketch *Beatrice Hannah of Gloster* has just arrived in St Ives Harbour, probably laden with coal from Lidney in the Forest of Dean. When the tide ebbs, her crew will toil at the dolly winch, heaving baskets of coal over the side to be delivered at £1 a cartload. (St Ives Archive – William Thomas Collection)

Until the 1950s coal fuelled the gasworks, power stations, industry and domestic heating. A friendly haze of coal smoke hovered over St Ives. The Liverpool coaster *Lady Thomas* discharges coal at Smeaton's Pier, two baskets at a time. (St Ives Archive – Major Butt Collection)

3

ST IVES – MINING

Rosewall Hill and Ransom United. Taken from Rosewall Hill, this extraordinary, late nineteenth-century photograph shows the extent of the mines that once dominated the upper part of St Ives. In the foreground are the engine houses of Rosewall Hill and Ransom United Mines, while in the Stennack Valley lie those of the celebrated St Ives Consols Mine. (David Elsbury)

Consols Mine. East Virgin headgear, St Ives Consols, c.1908. In the background (left) stands the church of St John in the Fields. St Ives Consols was founded by Sir Christopher Hawkins, MP, in 1818 as a means of strengthening his political power in the borough. James Halse, MP, took over the property in 1830 and constructed the nearby village of Halsetown to house his miners. Halse demanded absolute loyalty from his employees, who were only allowed to patronise establishments within which Halse had an interest. They were also required to vote for him! St Ives Consols (together with Trenwith and Giew Mine) was reworked by St Ives Consolidated Mines during 1907-1915. (Gerald Williams)

Trenwith Mine. Supervised by Captain Andrews (pictured right), workers at the British Radium Corporation's Trenwith Mine prepare to despatch pitchblende to their London factory for the extraction of radium. The company also had plans to turn St Ives into a health resort utilising the waters of the mine which were believed to have curative properties. Nothing came of these ideas but, for many years, the town of St Ives relied largely upon the radioactive waters of Trenwith to supplement its water supply. Trenwith's 1907 reworking was short-lived when contracts to sell radium to Germany became annulled following the outbreak of the First World War. (Private Collection)

North Wheal Providence Mine, *c. 1870*. Situated overlooking St Ives Harbour, the engine house of North Wheal Providence is a prominent feature in early photographs of the town. Its locality also made it a popular subject for artists in the late nineteenth century and, prior to its demolition in 1911, it briefly served as an artist's studio. The Pedn Olva Hotel now occupies this site. (St Ives Archive – Mary Dobbin Collection)

Wheal Ayr engine house, pictured left, was converted into a three-storey house before being demolished in 1935. The eight houses constructed on the site, now called Wheal Ayr Terrace, suffered subsidence in 2001, and their subsequent demolition two years later gave an expensive reminder of the mine workings that lie deep beneath the town. (St Ives Archive – Jeannette Harris Collection)

Providence Mine. The housing estates of Carbis Bay have long since buried much of the evidence of the mining industry that once prospered there. The prominent building in the left background was the mine's account house and still exists today in Count House Lane. (Gerald Williams)

Giew Mine. A group of miners at Frank's shaft, Giew Mine. Note the lumps of clay holding their candles in place on their hats. For a time, Giew was Cornwall's only active tin producer but, despite the miners agreeing to forfeit one-fifth of their monthly wage in order to sustain the property, the mine eventually succumbed to the falling price of tin in December 1922. (Gerald Williams)

Giew Mine in the process of being dismantled in 1923. Its closure marked the end of mining in the St Ives district, but the engine house survives as a striking memorial to an industry that once brought great prosperity to the town. (Gerald Williams)

4

ST IVES –
CHARACTERS & CUSTOMS

Percy Lane Oliver was born in St Ives at the home of his maternal grandparents. Percy was the founder, in 1921, of the Voluntary Blood Donor Service for the UK and was held in high esteem internationally for his work in this field of medicine. He is commemorated in the Stennack Surgery. (St Ives Stennack Surgery)

Tommy 'Chicky' Wedge was a St Ives fisherman who loved to play rugby. It was while he was playing for Cornwall that he was selected as scrum half for England. When Tommy arrived at the London ground, he was at first refused entry as he didn't look like the other players, dressed as he was in his 'best' navy fisherman's Guernsey and trousers and cap. The Cornish team represented England in the 1908 Summer Olympics against Australia and they came away with the silver medal. A draw was taken to see who should have it and Tommy won. For many years the medal was on display at St Ives Rugby Club. This portrait was painted by his daughter Catherine Bowtell. (Cathy Mckie)

John T. Barber and Cyril Noall were two sons of St Ives, much respected for their contributions to their county. 'Johnny' Barber wrote about a variety of subjects in his poems but the best loved by local folk are the poems about St Ives and its people. Many have a humorous bent and show his complete understanding of the human condition. Cyril Noall was a celebrated local historian with a vast knowledge of Cornwall and St Ives. He wrote many books about Cornwall including *The Book of St Ives* and *St Ives, Yesterday's Town*. Cyril was the curator of the St Ives Museum for twenty years. In 1959 both John and Cyril were made bards in the Gorsedd ceremony on the Island at St Ives. (Irene Tanner)

All towns have their well-known local characters. Eliza Uren is typical of many women living in Downlong in the late eighteenth and early nineteenth centuries. She carries home two large fish and wears a straw hat to keep the sun off her face. Over her skirt is a 'sogget', a hessian apron widely used by women working around the harbour. (St Ives Archive)

Colan Williams, known as 'Cully', was the choirmaster of Hellesveor Wesleyan Chapel. He was blind from a young age following an accident. He is remembered every Christmas in and around St Ives for his Christmas 'curls' (carols), the most famous of which is 'Hellesveor'. (St Ives Archive)

A familiar sight around the harbour during the middle of the last century was Ben Phillips with his horse, Captain, pulling the cart, under which ran Carlo, his dog. Ben was the last man to carry fish in this way. He would collect the catch from the fishing boats and then drive it to either the slipway market or to a waiting Newlyn lorry. (St Ives Archive)

Matt Pearce was a fruit and vegetable trader for the lower part of the town and is shown here in Back Road East. He sold his wares from the back of a flat bed cart pulled by his pony, Tommy. His cry of 'ripe tomatees' could be heard well in advance of his making an appearance. (Ross Barns)

Sir Edward Hain, his father, Edward, his son, Edward, and his daughters, Grace (standing) and Kate. Although trained as an accountant, Edward later came into the family shipping business on condition that it would purchase steamships. A total of eighty-seven ships were built for the Hain Line, mainly by J. Readhead & Sons of South Shields, one of the most outstanding owner/ builder associations in British shipbuilding history. All the ships carried the Cornish 'Tre' prefix, the first ship being the *Trewidden*. In 1900 Edward Hain was elected as the Liberal Unionist Member of Parliament for the Constituency of St Ives. In 1910 he was also elected President of the Chamber of Shipping. This was followed in 1912 by a knighthood. The Hain Shipping Line was sold to P&O after the death of Edward Hain's son at Gallipoli. (O'Riordan family)

Victorian Regatta. St Ives Swimming Races and Regatta, held every August, was a very popular event. The swimming and sailing were both taken very seriously with gritty competition for the Pazolt Cup, the Florence Cup and other awards and prizes. Here a late Victorian crowd, with the ladies in blouses and long skirts and the gentlemen in boaters and suits, waits for the action to begin from the beflagged committee boat. The outside of the swimming course is marked by more spectators in fishing gigs and skiffs. (Tim & Rita Lait Postcard Collection)

Opposite above: Midsummer Bonfire, 1964. The practice of celebrating Midsummer Eve goes back to pagan times. The revival took place in 1929 when a chain of bonfires was organised throughout the county of Cornwall. Folk dancing and a pasty supper are a must and the wording of the ceremony has been passed from generation to generation. To tread across the dying embers brings luck. Mayor Peter Tonks lights the bonfire. (St Ives Archive – Lee Sheldrake Collection)

Opposite below: Model boat sailing at Consols Pool, Good Friday. Dozens of St Ives families who value their heritage made their annual trek to Consols Pool on Good Friday morning to sail model boats. It is a tradition which dates back more than a century. The event pictured here enjoyed glorious weather but little wind, which meant that bamboo canes were very much in evidence to rescue stranded craft. In 2009 local people were enraged because this event had to be cancelled after funding to clear the pool was cut and health and safety concerns meant that volunteers could not pitch in to help. (Colin Sanger)

Above: John Knill celebrations, 1946. Born in Callington, Cornwall, John Knill was Customs Officer at St Ives from 1762-1782. Because of his love of St Ives, he wrote, 'My vanity prompted me to erect a mausoleum and to institute certain periodical return of a ceremony'. The ceremony takes place on St James' Day (25 July) every five years and John Knill was present at the first in 1801. Starting at the Guildhall, the procession of the Trustees, the Master of Ceremonies, the fiddler, the ten little girls and two widows, proceed to the Malakoff where they are transported to the Steeple. The event continues to this day. (George Ellis Collection, Kim Cooper, Cornish Studies Library)

Left: May Day, 2000. This ceremony was revived in 2000 by the then Mayor Chris Cocklin and his Consort Shirley Beck. Early records show that money was collected for the town's poor, and now, in a similar gesture, there are numerous charity stalls along the harbour front. This day-long event features a May Princess competition, Maypole dancing, the blowing of the May Day Horn, choruses of 'pee weeps' (handmade hollowed sticks) and a competition for decorated May sticks. (St Ives Archive – St Ives Camera Club)

Mayor Choosing, 1964. St Ives has had a Mayor since 1639, when the town was made a municipality by Charter of Charles I. Pictured are the Mayor Peter Tonks, Deputy Mayor Jack Couch and Mace Bearers, Willie and Kit Harry. The parade is passing the Market Place en route to the traditional service in the Parish Church. (St Ives Archive – Lee Sheldrake Collection)

Silver Ball, 1930. This event takes place on the first Monday after 3 February and is one of the few surviving games of hurling now played only by children. This early snap shows a short-lived attempt to provide a goal and rules for the proceedings. Nowadays the Mayor hurls the ball onto the beach and the winner usually passes the ball to a younger relative, to be returned to the Mayor at noon at the Guildhall when a gift is given. New pennies are also thrown for all the assembled children. This Feast Day celebrates the consecration of the Parish Church in 1434. (St Ives Archive – William Thomas Collection)

Left: Loving cup ceremony, 1981. Sir Francis Bassett of Tehidy used his influence to persuade Charles I to grant a Charter to the town. In 1640 he presented a beautiful, gilded-silver loving cup to commemorate this event. The inscription on the cup starts, 'Iff any discord twixt my frends shall arise, within the Burrough of Beloved St Ives, Itt is desyred that this my Cupp of Love, To Evrie one a Peace maker may Prove ...'. On Mayor Choosing Day in May, children are invited to take a sip from the cup and are given a saffron bun. This Mayor is Councillor Terry Tonkin. (*St Ives Times & Echo*)

Below: St Ives Carnival Week, 1959. This programme shows the many and varied events of Carnival Week, from art exhibitions to a dairy show. It is interesting to see that the carnival committee consisted of notable artists Malcolm Haylett and Clare White, and author S. Canynge Caple.

ST. IVES
CARNIVAL
WEEK
1–6 JUNE
1959

Programme—a brief outline of Events

MONDAY — Official Opening Ceremony. Studios open to the Public. Sculpture Exhibition opens in Penlee Gardens. Flower Show. Dramatic Society presents "Sailor Beware." Late evening Torchlight Procession.

TUESDAY — The Big Tuesday Show, in association with S.A.M.A. Alfred Wallis Exhibition opens.

WEDNESDAY — Lecture at Penwith Society of Arts. West of England Premiere "The Picasso Mystery" presented in association with the Arts Council. Dancing in the Streets. Old Tyme Ball at Guildhall. Barbeque on Porthgwidden Beach.

THURSDAY — Water Carnival. Mannequin Parade at Tregenna Castle. Cricket Match. Midnight Matinee at Royal Cinema.

FRIDAY — Dairy Show, Young Farmer's Display on Island. "Story of St. Ives" presented in Dramatic Form at Guildhall.

SATURDAY — The BIG CARNIVAL PARADE in Three Parts. Parade of Cornish Giants. St. Ives Cavalcade.—The Coming of the Artists. Carnival Dance.

- This is not the complete Programme, and does not include daily events such as the Painting Competition, Sports, Dog Shows, Band Concerts, to name but a few.

- This diverse six days has been devised and produced by the people of St. Ives and all profits will be given to the Cheshire Home for Incurables at Marazion.

Chairman & President — The Worshipful the Mayor of St. Ives (Councillor G. N. Pearce, J.P.)

Art Director ... Malcolm Haylett, L.S.I.A.
Hon. Carnival Secretary ... Miss Clare White
Hon. Treasurer ... William Doo
Press & Publicity ... S. Canynge Caple

All Enquiries to : The Carnival Office, Guildhall, St. Ives, Cornwall

5

ST IVES –
WRECKS & LIFEBOATS

The *Rosedale*, a large steamer bound for Cardiff from Southampton, ran aground on Porthminster Beach in a gale in 1893. The following night during a violent storm she broke in two. Using rocket apparatus, the sixteen crew were landed safely. The St Ives 'primitive' artist Alfred Wallis was charged with receiving brass, stolen from the ship by two youths, James Matthews Stevens and Richard T. Taylor. They were sent to Bodmin Gaol for a month and Wallis paid a £10 fine. He had pleaded not guilty but the brass was found hidden in a bag of bones in his storeroom. (Tim & Rita Lait Postcard Collection)

An early St Ives lifeboat had three names – *Moses*, *Covent Garden* and finally *Exeter*. She saved seventy-seven lives in twenty years. Here the second *Exeter*, which arrived in 1886, is rowing in the harbour with the local mackerel luggers on their moorings. (St Ives Archive – William Thomas Collection)

In this carefully posed Victorian portrait from around 1896, the second *Exeter* and her crew, complete with cork lifejackets, are ready for action. (St Ives Archive – John Ninnes Collection)

The French brigantine *Julien Marie* was bound for Bordeaux from Swansea with a cargo of coal when she was wrecked on Porthminster Beach on 19 February 1901. The crew were saved by the St Ives lifeboat *James Stevens No. 10*. (Private Collection)

The three-masted schooner *Enterprise* of Beaumaris, North Wales, was wrecked on the 'spits' by Hayle Bar on 11 September 1903. (St Ives Archive – Major Butt Collection)

The schooners *Mary Barrow* and *Lizzie R. Wilce* went aground on Porthminster Beach just a few hours apart during a storm in January 1908. Both ships were carrying coal from Swansea. The crews of both ships were rescued by the St Ives lifeboat *James Stevens*. The *Mary Barrow* returned to service and sailed for another twenty years before sinking off the Isle of Man. (Private Collection)

It often took over fifty men to launch St Ives' first motor lifeboat, *Caroline Parsons*, on station from 1933-1938. Not only did she have to be pulled along the wharf from the lifeboat house to the slipway but, when the tide was out, the men also had to haul her across the sand and wade into the sea before she was afloat. (St Ives Museum)

The ketch *Cicilia* was wrecked on the rocks behind the Arts Club on Westcott's Quay, 18 January 1935. (St Ives Archive – Major Butt Collection)

On 31 January 1938, the steamship *Alba*, a Panamanian-registered ship with a Hungarian and Yugoslavian crew, bound for Civitavecchia from Barry with a cargo of coal, was wrecked near the rocks on the Porthmeor side of the Island. The St Ives lifeboat *Caroline Parsons* went to her aid but capsized and ended up on the rocks. A small part of the *Alba* can still be seen at low tide. Five of the crew died and many were injured. (St Ives Archive – Major Butt Collection)

In June 1946 the steamship *Flowergate* grounded on Porthminster Beach, whilst under tow to a breakers yard. The 5,107-ton requisitioned German ship was later refloated to continue her final voyage. (St Ives Archive – Major Butt Collection)

The aptly named *Sand Runner*, a coaster from Goole, aground on Porthmeor Beach in May 1950. (St Ives Archive – Major Butt Collection)

On 30 September 1952, the minesweeper HMS *Wave* dragged her anchor in a westerly gale and ended up aground on the beach at Westcott's Quay. She was floated off with the aid of a barrage balloon inflated in the hull. (St Ives Archive – Major Butt Collection)

6

ST IVES –
RELIGION & EDUCATION

St Nicholas' Chapel. This prominent feature on the Island is not the original chapel which stood on the site and did not always have a religious use. The medieval building was taken over by the Preventive Service in the eighteenth century as a lookout to watch for smugglers. Later it became a military store, until the War Office no longer required it for that purpose. The chapel was in a poor state of repair so they demolished it in 1904, unaware of its local significance. This caused a local outcry and a prominent local resident, Sir Edward Hain, provided the money to rebuild the chapel, which is shown here nearing completion in 1911. Various renovations have been carried out since then, including one by J.F. Holman in 1971. (Tim & Rita Lait Postcard Collection)

St Ives Parish Church, *c.* 1890. Dedicated to St Ia and St Andrew, this fifteenth-century church was built with granite brought by sea from Zennor. Beside the church there is a late fifteenth-century cross, re-erected in 1850 having been found buried in the churchyard. The church tower, a prominent feature in the town, contains two bells which were cast in Hayle Foundry in 1830. Windows in the church were damaged in 1904 by an explosion in Hayle Dynamite Works. (Dr J. Ferguson)

New Connexion Chapel Harvest Festival, 1896. A Teetotal Society broke away from the Methodists and set up a church in Chapel Street in 1842. In 1860 the Society joined the New Connexion circuit, continuing to worship in this building until 1899, when they moved to a new church at the bottom of Bedford Road. The redundant chapel later became known as the Drill Hall. (St Ives Archive)

Zion Church choir. In 1786 the Countess of Huntingdon sent Revd Robert McCall to St Ives and in 1804 he converted an old fish cellar in Fore Street into the Zion Church, still in use today. Prior to this, he had preached in the open air or in the old Market House. The choirmaster William Jacobs, seated in the front, had the printing business further along Fore Street. Luke, his brother and business partner, attended Bedford Road Methodist Church. (Belinda Ratanyake)

Hellesveor Wesley Chapel. The choir and instrumentalists are posed for a group photograph outside the small chapel which had been built beside Consols Pool in 1844. It later became the Sunday school for the new chapel, which was built in 1937. The man in the second row, behind the young boy, is Colan 'Cully' Williams who was the choirmaster in the early 1900s. Cully Williams composed the famous Cornish carol 'Hellesveor'. (R.J. Noall, *Little Feathers and Stray Fancies*)

Catholic Church of Sacred Heart and St Ia. The foundation stone was laid on 27 February 1908 on the site at the top of Skidden Hill. It was built with local stone from Trelyon Downs for a total cost of £4,000 and was officially opened in September 1908. Many artists and local people were critical of the fact that its copper-covered spire and red tiles were not traditional building materials, making it stand out amongst the slate rooftops of the town. (Private Collection)

Left: Father Austin W. Delaney, 1950s. He was a Benedictine monk who came to St Ives on sick leave and stayed on as the priest at St Ives Catholic Church from 1937-1972. Father Delaney was a much-loved and respected member of the community, ministering to people regardless of their beliefs. In 1973 he was given the Freedom of the Borough, in honour of his long service and his esteemed position in the community. Here he is bidding farewell to the Ellis family who were about to emigrate to the USA. (Ellis Family Collection)

Below: Board School. Designed by Silvanus Trevail, it was built for the sum of £4,450 on farmland beside the Stennack. The school opened in January 1881, with separate departments for boys, girls and infants. Education was compulsory but not free. Fees were 2*d* per week for infants and 3*d* for older children, or 2*d* each for siblings. The first headmaster was Thomas Kay, who achieved excellent results despite problems caused by rivalry between Uplong and Downlong children. This picture shows the back of the school, with Trenwith Burrows' spoil heaps from the mine on the other side of the Stennack and Trenwith Square top right. (The Late Matthew Farrell Collection)

Infant class, *c.* 1951. These children are in their classroom in the infants' school. On the left, some have their hands in the water tray and those on the right in the sand tray. In 1966 the infants moved up to a new school on Trenwith Burrows. After the juniors also moved out to a new school, the building became redundant. Over a period of years there were proposals that it could become the 'Tate of the West' but eventually it opened in 1991 as the Stennack Surgery. (St Ives Archive)

Island Road School boys' class. A bell rang out over Downlong to summon these children to the school, which opened in 1896. The school was used for less than fifty years and closed on 7 June 1940, although it was occasionally opened for evacuee children during the war. In addition to this, it served as an emergency cooking centre after a bomb was dropped on the town's gasworks in August 1942. The building is now a community centre. (St Ives Archive)

Chy-an-Chy, 1890s. Prior to the building of the Board School, children could receive a basic education at one the 'dame schools' in the town. An example of this was near the Wharf, in the cottage with the bow window, in which an elderly lady taught Downlong children for *2d* per week. For those who could afford more, there were academies, such as James Rowe's school which stood beside Academy Steps. This academy was one of the schools attended by Edward Hain, founder of the Hain Steamship Co. (Tim & Rita Lait Postcard Collection)

St Ives Library, 1936. Another aspect of education is the provision of a library and this image, with the turret gaily festooned, is probably from the time of the coronation of George VI. The foundation stone of St Ives Library was laid in 1896 by the donor, philanthropist John Passmore Edwards, a wealthy Cornish-born newspaper proprietor. The site was given by local MP, T.B. Bolitho, and the architects were Messrs Symons & Son of Blackwater. For many years the library shared the building with the St Ives Museum but the museum moved to Wheal Dream, its current location, in 1951. The library has been totally remodelled twice in its over 100-year history. The first time was in 1968, when the architect was H.C. Gilbert, and more recently in 2006. Each transformation has reflected the needs of a modern library. (St Ives Archive – Jeannette Harris Collection)

7

ST IVES –
TOURISM & BEACHES

St Ives Harbour, early 1900s. Before the advent of tourism, most of the buildings around the harbour were associated with the fishing industry and few visitors ventured along the Wharf. However, it became a popular promenade after the completion of Wharf Road in 1922. The sail lofts, net lofts and boatyards were gradually converted into artists' studios, shops and cafes. This trend has continued and the Wharf area is now almost entirely focused on the holiday industry. (Tim & Rita Lait Postcard Collection)

St Ives Station, 1906. The St Ives branch line was opened on 24 May 1877 and the first regular goods service began four days later. In the following week, on 1 June, the first passenger train steamed into the station. The railway was instrumental in the development of St Ives as a holiday resort, bringing in visitors to stay in the town and also day trippers, many of whom would spend the day on the nearby Porthminster Beach. (Tim & Rita Lait Valentine Postcard Collection)

Porthminster Beach. Possibly taken on a regatta day, the beach is crowded with people – all fully clothed, unlike nowadays. Behind the tents are seine boats and beyond them is the Pavilion, also known as the Tin House or Tin Tabernacle. Many locals and visitors were very critical of this unattractive, galvanized structure which had been erected in 1913, but it provided a much-needed venue for summer entertainment until sold for scrap in 1922 for £32. (Tim & Rita Lait Postcard Collection)

Porthmeor Beach, early 1900s. Until 1893 there had been no easy access but the construction of a road gave visitors a promenade above the beach and by the early 1900s there were bathing machines for hire. Until around 1900, visitors to the beach would have been deterred by the dumping of ashes from the adjacent gasworks, now the site of the Tate Gallery, and by the danger from blasting in Carthew Quarry, near Man's Head. (Tim & Rita Lait Postcard Collection)

Porthmeor Beach, 1930s. John Care became the proprietor of the Island end of Porthmeor in 1912 and in the following year he put an advertisement in the *St Ives Times*, claiming it to be one of the finest bathing beaches in Cornwall. The advert stated that 'being open to the broad Atlantic, the water is fresh, very buoyant and free from objectionable taints'. By the 1930s there were refreshment facilities, together with tents and deckchairs for hire, at both ends of the beach. (Tim & Rita Lait Postcard Collection)

Advertisement for Porthminster Beach. This appeared in the 1940 *St Ives and District Guide*, extolling the virtues of the beach. Further on in the same guide there was an advert for Porthmeor, the 'best and safest bathing beach in Cornwall', with 'splendid putting and bowling greens overlooking the beach' and a car park. Thus the beaches were competing to attract visitors.

Porthgwidden, 1890s. In the seventeenth and eighteenth centuries, Porthgwidden Cove on the east side of the Island was the main landing place for fishing boats, guided in at night by a lantern on Lamp Rock, now the site of the Coastwatch station. Buildings in this picture include bark-houses, for preserving fishing nets, and a kipper house, with its three distinctive chimneys. Separate areas of grass on the Island were used for grazing and for drying 'barked' nets and washing. (Tim & Rita Lait Valentine Postcard Collection)

Porthgwidden Beach, 1940s. The meadow above the beach is being used as a campsite, with a couple of caravans on higher ground. Tents were not necessarily occupied by visitors; some were used by local children whose mothers let out their rooms during the summer. Camping cost 1s 3d per night in 1940 but it was only 1s per week for the local children. The beach was relatively undeveloped until permanent beach chalets were built in 1954-1955. (Tim & Rita Lait Postcard Collection)

St Ives Harbour, 1930s. The vessels in the harbour include sailing boats which, together with rowing boats, were available for hire. These yachts would have competed in the annual St Ives Regatta, which took place off Porthminster Beach. The harbour foreshore, once tainted with fish waste, is now a very popular beach. (The Late Clive Carter Collection)

Wharf Road, 1920s. Men are gutting and packing fish on the wharf whilst beyond them, in contrast, is a group of well-dressed ladies. Scavenging seagulls have long been part of the harbour scene, shown here feeding on the fish waste. As this became unavailable, the gulls turned to stealing food out of people's hands and from waste bins. (Tim & Rita Lait Postcard Collection)

CRIMSON TOURS

Luxuriously Appointed
Coaches   Run   Daily

To Land's End, Lizard, Newquay, Falmouth, Clovelly, Tintagel, Looe, Fowey, Lamorna Cove, Etc. ——

(FULL DETAILS ON APPLICATION)

7 & 14 Seaters for Private Hire
Any Distance.   Moderate Terms

LANDAULETS and TOURING CARS

Booking Office: "CRIMSON TOURS"
The Terrace, St. Ives. 'PHONE 45

BLEWETT'S GARAGE

STENNACK, St. Ives

Fully Equipped Garage Accommodation and
Lock-Ups.   'Phone 45

Advertisement for Crimson Tours. This appeared in an official St Ives handbook in the 1920s. At that time most holidaymakers came down on the train; therefore, the only way they could see other parts of Cornwall was by means of coach tours. However, the company also catered for those with cars by providing garage accommodation.

Wharf Road, 1940s. On the left is the garage of Stevens Tours, another one of the coach companies providing trips around Cornwall and beyond. Part of the Harbour Cafe had been an artist's studio and prior to that it was a sail loft. Further along is another cafe, the Copper Kettle, beneath which there had been an ice store. (Tim & Rita Lait Postcard Collection)

The Cornish Belle, 1950s. This boat, shown here at Seal Island, west of St Ives, was one of the motor boats providing trips for holidaymakers. She later became the fishing boat *Sister Theresa* and was replaced by another, larger, *Cornish Belle*. Pleasure boats of various types still go to Seal Island and some also take people out on short fishing trips. (Tim & Rita Lait Postcard Collection)

8

ST IVES – THE ARTS

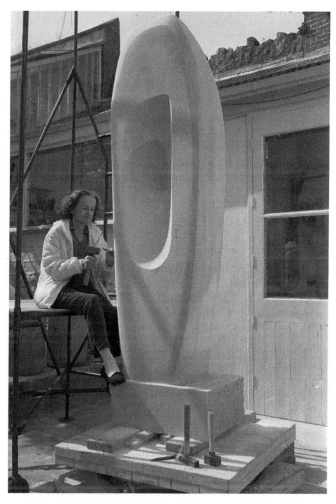

Dame Barbara Hepworth (1903-1975) carving her stone sculpture 'Vertical Form' in the yard at Trewyn Studio. Barbara Hepworth bought the studio with its secluded, walled garden in 1949 and there she lived and worked for the rest of her life. In 1968, she and the potter Bernard Leach received the Freedom of St Ives; the citation described the sculptor as being 'a truly eminent artist living and working in the community'. (St Ives Archive – Lee Sheldrake Collection)

A view of Barnoon Cemetery overlooking Porthmeor Beach, with St Nicholas' Chapel on the Island in the distance. In the foreground is the grave of the artist and mariner Alfred Wallis, who died in 1942. The unique gravestone was made from tiles decorated by Bernard Leach. It illustrates the artist ascending the stairs of a lighthouse, one of Wallis's most frequently depicted motifs. (St Ives Archive – Stella Redgrave Collection)

From the 1880s a number of artists set up painting schools in St Ives. These introduced generations of students from around the world to landscape and seascape painting, and later to non-figurative art. Each summer, between 1955 and 1960, the Cornish-born artist Peter Lanyon advertised for students to attend 'St Peter's Loft Art School', in a traditional building on Back Road West. Here he is shown, wearing his beret, giving advice to one of his students. (St Ives Archive – Stella Redgrave Collection)

The potter Bernard Leach attaching a handle to a jug at the Leach Pottery, March 1971. Bernard Leach is often referred to as 'the father of modern studio pottery'. Having learnt his craft in Japan early in the twentieth century, he and his colleague Shoji Hamada opened a pottery on the outskirts of St Ives in 1920. There Leach succeeded in recapturing some of the values of the traditional craftsman. The Leach Pottery has recently been restored and re-opened to the public. (Marjorie Parr Collection, photo by Peter Kinnear)

Left: An amateur painter, Miss Aycliffe, at her easel below the West Pier in 1914, is being watched by a group of local boys. Artists were a regular sight around the town; the clear air and extraordinary light were important reasons for them to come to this remote part of Cornwall and work outdoors. However, no one was allowed to paint on a Sunday; easels would be knocked to the ground if an artist was found to be working on the Sabbath. (St Ives Archive)

Below: Packers working at Lanhams' picture framing department in 1944, preparing paintings for shipment by train for the current exhibition at the Royal Academy of Arts in London. The business was founded in High Street by the entrepreneur James Lanham (1848-1931) who, from the mid-1880s, also provided the artists in St Ives with their first public gallery and high quality artist materials, as well as selling wine, spirits and tobacco. (St Ives Archive)

Borlase Smart painting the rocky Cornish coastline, probably in the 1930s. Born in 1881, Smart first moved to St Ives in 1913 and lived most of his life in the town until his untimely death in 1947. He was not only an important painter of seascapes but he played a major role in the life of the town itself. Secretary of the St Ives Society of Artists for many years, Smart understood the importance of the young, modern artists moving into St Ives in the 1940s and encouraged them to exhibit with the society. The Porthmeor Studios and the Penwith Society of Arts are both dedicated to his memory. (Brian Smart Collection)

The image above is the remains of the St Ives Gasworks facing Porthmeor Beach, as it looked in 1967 when gas was no longer being produced. A contractor is starting to construct a turning space to accommodate the newly planned, one-way traffic system in the town. (St Ives Archive)

In 1993 the site was transformed into Tate St Ives to celebrate the Modernist legacy of the town's international artist colony. Designed by Eldred Evans and David Shalev, the gallery welcomes thousands of visitors each year. Its entrance loggia reflects the shape and size of the old gas holder, and from its rooftop restaurant there is a spectacular view of St Ives Bay. (Jason Sugden)

9

HALSETOWN

Halsetown Inn was completed in 1831 by James Halse for his model village. On 29 December that year, Mrs Catherine Hodge was appointed the first 'landlord'. The inn soon became popular with local tin miners, James Halse using it as the wage office. After receiving their meagre wage in the room below, the miners passed into the public bar where the landlady pinned salt fish to the beams to give them a thirst. The inn was the hub of the village, being used for local petty sessions, hunt and 'ticketing' meetings where the local mines agents would present samples of tin ore to the smelting companies. They wrote on tickets the price they offered. The highest offer was accepted by the Mines' Chairman, James Halse. Today it is a popular venue, and James Halse's mounting stone and auctioneer's plinth can still be seen. (St Ives Museum)

Sliding rock. This granite outcrop behind the top row of cottages in Halsetown was worn smooth by generations of children who used to climb to the top and slide down. One of these children was Henry Irving (1838-1905), then known as Johnny Broadrib who, at the age of four, came to live in the village with his aunt and uncle. He later became a famous actor and was the first to receive a knighthood. Irving was reputedly the inspiration for the title character in Bram Stoker's *Dracula*. On his last visit to the village he reputedly stood on the rock gazing out over the countryside, as if bidding farewell. (St Ives Archive – Erica Sutcliffe)

Above: The new Parish Church of St John in the Fields was built on a site in Hellesvean, about one mile from the village of Halsetown. This was because the land nearer the centre of the village was owned by Nonconformists who refused, on sectarian grounds, to sell the land. The church was designed by J.P. St Aubyn and was consecrated on 26 May 1860 by Bishop Phillpotts of Exeter. James Halse's brother-in-law, Robert Hichens, provided the site and £1,000 endowment towards the cost. The first incumbent was the Reverend W.H. Drake, who had nine children. The old vicarage was built for him. The longest serving vicar was the Reverend Barfett, from 1916 to 1968. In the early 1970s, a central altar was installed and the pews replaced by chairs. (Tim & Rita Lait Postcard Collection)

Left: Revd Barfett was a rugged countryman and enthusiastic gardener who visited his parishioners on a motorbike. In 1956, when the vicarage was renovated, oil lamps were replaced by electricity. During the Second World War the church and vicarage were damaged by bombs. With Revd Barfett is Miss Noye, the last teacher at Halsetown School, which closed in 1966. (St Ives Archive)

At Bussow, near Halsetown, stands this thirteenth-century dovecote or culver house. Built of granite with very thick walls, it has a domed beehive roof and a low doorway. The pigeons flew in through small holes about 5ft from the ground. The birds, eaten by the local lord, grew fat on grain from his tenants' fields. (Dr J. Ferguson)

10

CARBIS BAY & LELANT

CARBIS BAY,

Carbis Bay Station. On 1 June 1877, the Great Western Railway opened Carbis Bay Station on their new St Ives to St Erth branch line. This subsequently became the name for the village, which developed from three or four nearby hamlets. The line was the last to be built using Brunel's broad gauge, later converting to standard gauge in 1892. Here, the saddle tank train leaving Carbis Bay is heading for St Erth, carrying both passengers and goods. (St Ives Archive)

Seine fishing. Long before Carbis Bay became a 'holiday playground' it was, in fact, a minor fishing beach. Alongside the Carbis Bay Hotel on the beach stood bollards and several capstans where fishing boats could be moored. There were also several little stone huts which acted as shelter for the fishermen. The postcard, from around 1900, shows seine fishing, where a huge net was cast around a shoal of fish and gathered up to bring in the catch, as described on page 21. (St Ives Archive – Jeannette Harris Collection)

Carbis Bay Hotel, *c.* 1890. With the coming of the railway, a new era of prosperity for tourism was ushered in. Carbis Bay Hotel was constructed over old mine workings on the edge of the beach, thus providing much needed accommodation for the summer visitors at the end of the nineteenth century. The hotel was built to the design of the well-known Cornish architect Silvanus Trevail in 1894. In the distance can be seen Treloyhan Manor, another of Trevail's creations. (St Ives Archive – Jeannette Harris Collection)

The Village, *c.* 1900. The postcard shows the Longstone area of Carbis Bay. During the 1930s, it was decided to widen St Ives Road. The most notable change was at Longstone, whereby some of the buildings belonging to Longstone Farm, shown on the right, were removed to make way for a wider corner at the junction with Porthrepta Road. (Private Collection)

Carbis Bay Beach, *c.* 1900. Donkey rides were a particular feature of Carbis Bay Valley and sands in the early decades of the twentieth century. The donkeys, which were owned by Mr J. Payne, gave rides and also pulled a chariot along the beach and tea gardens. The principal customers were children on Sunday school tea treats. The price of the ride was 1*d* per person. (Tim & Rita Lait Postcard Collection)

Payne's Tea Gardens and Amusements, *c.* 1930. During the 1930s, the Payne's Tea Gardens, which were set up in the previous century, proved to be as popular as ever. They attracted locals, choir outings, day visitors, Sunday school tea treats and holiday visitors from afar, to sample the leisure amenities. The largest room, Payne's Dining Hall, shown here, was a venue for dances, roller skating and church gatherings. (Tim & Rita Lait Postcard Collection)

Payne's Boating Lake, *c.* 1930. After the 1920s, Payne's transformed a former mine pool area into a boating lake where, for a precious sixpence, one could row a little wooden boat around the shallow muddy waters. (Private Collection)

An advert for Carbis Bay Tea Rooms. (Private Collection)

Roach's Garage, situated at the entrance to Carbis Bay, provided a much needed service to the people of St Ives and Carbis Bay. This fine, distinctive building is sadly no longer standing, having been demolished in 2004 to make way for flats now known as Roach's Court. (Private Collection)

In 1964, Longstone Cemetery was consecrated. The service was taken by the Bishop of Truro, Revd Graham Leonard, assisted by Canon A.S. Roberts. In attendance were W. Rainey Edwards, Town Clerk and Councillors Ashby, Jory and Archie Knight. There is a fine Barbara Hepworth sculpture, 'Ascending Form (Gloria)', at the entrance. (St Ives Archive – Lee Sheldrake Collection)

Lelant ferry hut, 1916. Over the centuries Lelant is thought to have had ferries at several points along the Hayle Estuary to assist travellers across the treacherous sands. One was at the site of Lelant Station, at the bottom of what is now called Station Hill, but known as Quay Lane until the early twentieth century. The one shown in this photograph is just to the north of St Uny Church, on the edge of the golf course.

The job of the ferryman included maintaining and lighting the navigation lights along the channel into Hayle Harbour, so that vessels would not ground on the sand bar.

Thomas Gall (1807-1890) was the first known ferryman at this crossing and the job was handed down in his family through grandsons and sons-in-law. The ferryman in this 1916 photograph is Tom Pomeroy, ferryman from 1911 to 1932. He was the brother-in-law of Thomas Gall Whatty, Thomas Gall's grandson.

Ferry trade was brisk until the end of the First World War, but then began to decline due to the increase in motor traffic using Hayle Causeway, which had been built in the 1820s. It is salutary to think that if sea level predictions are correct, Penwith will be an island by 2050 and ferries will again be necessary. (Lelant History Trust – Cornish Studies Library)

Lelant Station, 1905. The St Erth to St Ives branch line, opened in 1877, gave its passengers a panoramic view of St Ives Bay before they reached their destination. Prematurely lamented by Flanders and Swann in their 1960s song 'Slow Train', it survived Beeching's axe and is still operating today.

This photograph shows a saddle tank locomotive with engineer and fireman, and the station staff. The gentleman in uniform with a tail coat in the centre of the platform is probably Mr John Hosking, the stationmaster.

Notice the gent with moustache and top hat looking out of the first carriage. Is he keen to be recorded for posterity or annoyed that his arrival at St Ives has been delayed by the then lengthy process of photography? (Lelant History Trust – Cornish Studies Library)

Funeral procession approaching St Uny Church, Lelant. This grand funeral procession must have been for a person of some social standing, who died at about the end of the nineteenth century. The priest, third from left, in a biretta and with a white beard, is the Revd R.F. Tyacke, vicar of Lelant from 1869 to 1901, and founder of the West Cornwall Golf Club. Notice the absence of women and girls, the universal wearing of hats, including the robed crucifer and choir, and the horse-drawn hearse followed by mourners at the rear. (Lelant History Trust – Cornish Studies Library)

Lelant Fair, 10 August 1908. According to Hobson Matthews' *History of St Ives, Lelant, Towednack and Zennor*, in 1295 Edward I granted to William Bottreaux the privilege of holding a weekly Thursday market within his manor of La Nant. The same Charter granted two fairs on the feasts of the Purification and the Assumption of the Blessed Virgin, 2 February and 15 August. The market disappeared over time, but Lelant Fair is again mentioned in 1792 and was an annual event during the nineteenth and early twentieth centuries. Early on it was a market with sales of livestock and local produce, rather like our present-day farmers' markets, but by the early twentieth century amusements were becoming more popular. This photograph shows the fair being held at the lower end of Church Lane with St Uny Church in the background. Stalls selling produce are on the left of the road, with some amusements on the right. In the background, to the right, an activity is taking place on the Winnowing Green. The group of young people in the centre foreground, wearing their Sunday best, are enjoying the novelty of having their photographs taken. The February fair may have been replaced by Lelant's Patronal Feast, which is still celebrated annually in late January or early February, on the Sunday nearest to 2 February, the Feast of the Purification. (Lelant History Trust – Cornish Studies Library)

Opposite above: Lelant Post Office. During the last quarter of the nineteenth century, Lelant Post Office was run by Charles Polkinghorne Burt and his family. Originally a tailor, Charles Burt, seen here seventh from the left, was also a Methodist lay preacher at the Primitive Methodist Chapel (now Lelant Village Hall; gable end visible top left of picture). His wife, Mary Jane, in the large white apron, was his assistant, and his daughter, Mary Sarah, was telegraphist; son Harry was postman, and youngest son, Albert, was telegraph messenger. It truly was a family business.

The site of the Post Office at this time was in the property called Eastleigh, now a private residence, and opposite the modern Post Office which was, sadly, recently closed. (Lelant History Trust – Cornish Studies Library)

Opposite below: Abbey Hill, Lelant, 1906. In marked contrast to the busy road through Lelant today, this photograph depicts the peacefulness of Lower Lelant in the early years of the twentieth century. On the left, a young man in a cap, Norfolk jacket and knickerbockers poses outside the Court House, while across the road, in front of Trendreath House, stands a gentleman in a wide-brimmed hat, carrying his jacket. This photograph is dated November 1906, which must have been an exceptionally warm month.

In the centre background is the Abbey, the oldest property in the village after the church. In his 1892 *History of St Ives, Lelant, Towednack and Zennor*, Hobson Matthews describes it as the clergy house of Lelant prior to the Reformation. Be that as it may, it dates from the late fifteenth or early sixteenth centuries and contains a chamber said to be a priests' hole. Rumours of smugglers and a tunnel to the coast survive to the present. (Lelant History Trust – Cornish Studies Library)

Armistice Day Service at Lelant war memorial, *c.* 1925. Like every village and town in the country, Lelant lost young men in the First World War. The war memorial, seen here on Armistice Day in around 1925, lists the names of eight soldiers and one sailor. In such a small community, this loss would be widely felt, hence the gathering on this day would comprise most of the village. The service was conducted by the vicar, Revd Arthur G. Chapman, seen to the left of the picture, and the Methodist minister, in gown and mortarboard, to the right. The Lelant Village Band, far left, provided the music. The obviously inclement November weather had not reduced the number of those gathered to remember. (Lelant History Trust – Cornish Studies Library)

In this tranquil scene from July 1940, a waterside picnic is enjoyed at Lelant. A steam coaster sails up the estuary, probably with coal for Hayle Power Station. On the shore an old St Ives lugger serves as a house boat. The small rowing boat is the Lelant to Hayle ferry. (Lelant History Trust – Cornish Studies Library)

11

HAYLE

The Paddington to Penzance express train crossing Hayle Viaduct in 1953. Beneath Brunel's 1852 viaduct was the site of Hayle's original railway station, built in 1837. The Isis Memorial Garden, dedicated to the town's lifeboat, was planted under the viaduct in 1993. (Ronnie Williams Postcard Collection)

Foundry Square, taken in 1910 in front of Harvey's Market House. In the 1920s, after the foundry closed, the building was converted into the Palace cinema. Partially destroyed by fire in 1935, the remaining building, now single-storey, is a Lloyds TSB Bank. (Hayle Archive)

Penpol Terrace, 1904. The railway track of the original Hayle Railway can still be seen. This line was opened in 1837 to carry goods, although passengers were also catered for, from Harvey's Foundry via the Cornish Copper Co. Foundry to Redruth, with spur lines to Porteath and Tresavean Mine at Lanner. It was abandoned in the 1850s when Brunel's Great Western Railway line was built. (Hayle Archive)

Left: Hayle's first farm shop was built into the wall of the former Penpol Hammer Mill on Foundry Hill in the 1960s. The section of the wall was rebuilt in 1987 when the Hammer Mill was converted into Millpond Gardens, now a local amenity area. (Ronnie Williams Collection)

Below: Inner Millpond Pool, Hayle, 1906. The photograph shows the pool when it was used as an ornamental lake for the town villas along Millpond Avenue. Caspian pond turtles were put into the Millpond in the early 1900s and were certainly still living there in 2004, over 100 years later. The Millponds are now an urban nature reserve. (Hayle Archive)

St Michael's Hospital, Downes House. An aerial view of the house built in 1880 for William Rawlings by the Cornish architect, John Dando Sedding. It is in the top left-hand corner of the picture. The house was for many years a convent, housing the nuns who managed St Michael's Hospital. It is now a residential home.

An aerial view from the 1960s. The development of Hayle depended upon communications – the town had a canal, a steam ship service and, of course, roads and a railway. Its first railway opened in 1837, which was then superseded by Brunel's Plymouth to Penzance line (1852), seen here with the road snaking its way under the viaduct twice. The Turnpike Causeway across the estuary (1825) provided a more direct link than the ancient road from Angarrack to St Erth.

A 1932 aerial view of Copperhouse. The 1842 tidal mill is still standing, as is the Methodist Chapel and its school house. The tidal mill was demolished in 1936 and the chapel is now Pool's Court housing estate. The large white building in the centre is the remains of the Phoenix works, the Cornish Copper Co. building. Industry in Hayle started to grow in the eighteenth century when a group of Camborne copper smelters moved to Hayle in 1756 to take advantage of the estuary. When in 1779 John Harvey moved to Hayle, the Copper Co. had rights over all the quays and he had great difficulty in landing his cargos. For a time he had to use lighters moored in the estuary where cargos would be landed and small boats would take them to a beach landing area. (Hayle Archive)

A quiet day in Fore Street, Copperhouse, December 1971. (Hayle Archive)

The cobbler's shop of J. Symonds & Sons in Chapel Lane stood opposite Copperhouse Methodist Chapel. (Ronnie Williams Collection)

The Lethlean Clapper Bridge built by Revd William Hockin Senior, the rector of Phillack Church in 1812. His initials and the date are carved on the lintel spanning the leat and next to it is a Harvey's boundary stone with 'H1' carved on it. (Andrew Szmidla)

The Church of St Piala and St Felicitas at Phillack was originally built in 1257. Its fifteenth-century bell tower houses a fine peal of eight bells. A very early form of a 'Chi-Rho' symbol can be found above the main door. A substantial internal rebuild took place in 1856. St Piala has a holy well sited in the garden opposite the church. This picture was taken before the road was realigned in 1973.

The Bucket of Blood public house in Churchtown, Phillack. Dating from the eighteenth century, it is built on the site of a medieval pilgrim's inn and the nearby Sanctuary Fields. The route down to the river ford to Lelant was waymarked with crosses, one of which still remains on Mexico Towans.

The Cove, Hayle, 1920s. A path leads down past the Cove Cafe to what was known as the 'paddling pool', in which children could play safely in the water. One of the placards beside the hut is advertising Cornish wrestling, organised by the *Daily News*. It is interesting to note that the cafe had a telephone for public use. (Hayle Archive)

Looking towards St Ives from Hayle Towans, 1927. The area known as the Towans (Cornish for dunes) is bordered by three miles of golden sands, stretching to Godrevy. There are a few houses near the edge of the dunes but, just as today, most of the accommodation is for holidaymakers. The majority of visitors would have travelled down on the train but a few came by road, in cars such as this little Austin. (Tony Pratt Postcard Collection)

BUSINESS & INDUSTRY

Harvey & Co. coppersmith's workshops at Viaduct Yard, pictured from the Plantation. They were demolished in 1983. (Virginia Bliss)

On the left are the newly built showrooms of UBM Harvey, pictured in 1974 following the fire which destroyed their main offices. The building in the foreground is the Coppersmith's Shop, one of the last remaining workshops of the Harvey's Foundry complex, demolished in 1984. (Virginia Bliss)

Marine engines in Cornwall Electric Power Co. fitting shop in the 1890s. (Virginia Bliss)

Jabus Bickel Junior and his wife on their tandem tricycle. Jabus followed his father, Jabus Bickel Senior, as chief engineer at Harvey & Co. and this splendid machine was made to his own design. (Hayle Archive)

Hayle Power Station, built in 1910 for the Cornish Power Co., on the left with the two chimneys and the ICI plant on the right of the picture, later to become Associated Octel, which opened in 1939. ICI produced an anti-knock ingredient for aviation fuel based on bromine distilled from sea water. Both companies closed in the late 1970s. (Chris Quick)

Unloading coal at the Power Station Wharf. The overhead coal conveyor can be seen in the background. The small, white building and the conveyor in the foreground were used for sulphur storage. (Hayle Archive)

J. & F. Pool's staff and lorry in Market Square, 1924. This company was started by two brothers, James and Frederic Pool, in 1862 and produced perforated plate and other services to industry. J. & F. Pool were taken over by Cooper Industries Group PLC in 1987, then in 1995 they were taken over by Ash & Lacy PLC. These companies kept trading under the Pool's name until the early twenty-first century. (Virginia Bliss)

Loggans Mill when it was part of the milling company, Hosken, Trevithick & Polkinghorne. The mill was rebuilt after a fire in 1850 and was the last of a series of mills which had occupied this site since the ninth century. It was listed in the Domesday Survey of 1086 as Connerton Mill. Loggans Mill was sold to Spillers in 1930 and finally closed in the 1960s. (Hayle Archive)

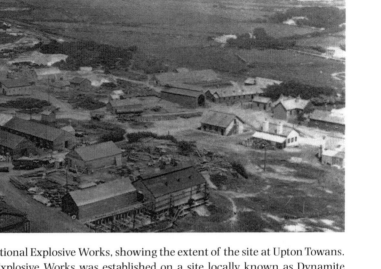

An aerial view of the National Explosive Works, showing the extent of the site at Upton Towans. In 1888 the National Explosive Works was established on a site locally known as Dynamite Towans. Originally built to supply the mining industry with the new nitroglycerine-based explosives, it soon grew to supply the military and during the First World War employed about 2,000 people. The remote location on the Towans proved a wise move as there were a number of accidents resulting in explosions. Four workers were killed in 1904 in an explosion so powerful it was heard as far away as Truro. The company closed in the 1920s. (The Bate Collection)

Mr H.E. Bate, the manager of the National Explosive Works. (The Bate Collection)

The National Explosive Works Power Station at Upton Towans. The site was used for storage by ICI until the 1960s. (The Bate Collection)

A worker in the National Explosive Works' glycerine nitrating house H3. This stood on the highest point of the site known as 'Jack Straw Hill'. The name came from a priest who took part in the Peasants' Revolt in 1381. (The Bate Collection)

The ladies of the National Explosive Works. Munitions workers were often nicknamed 'canaries' because of the yellow pigmentation of their hands, from the cordite used in making the explosives. (Virginia Bliss)

CHARACTERS

A street scene photographed in the early 1900s beneath Angarrack Viaduct. (Don Guiver)

St John's Street. 1910. The street traders would sell fish, fresh fruit and vegetables, logs and small household items to local residents from their donkey carts. (Hayle Archive)

Above: The bell ringers of Phillack Church in 1978. From left to right, back row: R. Thomas, M. Thomas, S. Thomas, M. Smaldon (Capt.), R. Radcliffe, G. Hawke. Third row: I. Watson, Miss P. Fisher, Mrs D. Hagan, Mrs E. Thomas, S. Richards. Second row: S. Green, Revd F. Canham, Revd J. Elford, Mrs A. Elford, Lt Cdr R. Coombe (Church Warden), Revd G. Bennett. Front row: S. Hagan, R. Abbey, B. Daniel. (Ronnie Williams Collection)

Opposite above: Hayle ladies cricket team in the 1950s. From left to right, back row: Jean Cock, Eileen Wherry, Steve Bond, Clarice Wherry, Marjorie Richards. Middle row: Phyllis Drew, Rita Cattan, Barbara Coombe, Elizabeth Bond, Evelyn Letcher. Front row: June Sleeman, Betty Reynolds. (Chris Quick)

Opposite below: Hayle Old Boys rugby team in the 1954/55 season. The person standing fourth from the left is Rick Rescorla, the hero of the 9/11 Twin Towers attacks in New York. He was in charge of Morgan Stanley's security when the attacks took place.

From left to right, back row: Frankie Mills, Geoffrey Burgan, Clifford Toman, Rick (Tammy) Rescorla, Terry Mungles, Jimmy Hosking, Roger Peak, Tony Hosking, Nino Thomas. Middle row: Phillip Richards, Kingsley Williams, Frankie Johns, Brian Bray, Norman Thomas, Geoffrey Mungles. Front row: Vivian Philp, Michael (Tripe) Thomas. (Chris Quick)

Hayle 1st XV rugby team in 1946/47. From left to right, back row: Mr Baumbach, George Lowther, Jack Bassett, Jack Gunn, Tino Thomas, Charlie Daniels, Ronnie Baumbach, Stanley Sullivan, Ernie (Tracy) Granville, Freddie Sampson, Charlie Penrose, Bob Philp, William Murt. Middle row: Reggie Hosking, Sammy Hosken, Frank (Di) Trewartha, Aubrey Jones, Lennard Rowe, Ellis Polkinghorne. Front row: Donald Irish, Norman Thomas, Lionel Irish. (Chris Quick)

Hayle cricket team in about 1961. From left to right, back row: Alan Chapman, Vic Sparks, Cyril Trembath, Kenneth Lang, Roger Chapman, Colin Polglase, Sidney Perry, John Burrows, Trevor Lang. Front row: Wilson Williams, Hewart Hosking, Trevor (Shep) Pellow, Frankie Johns, Ken Pavey. Seated: David Gilbert. (Chris Quick)

Copperhouse Methodist Chapel choir, 1895. Back row: fifth from left, no hat, Dr Pearce (Doctor of Music). Front row: second from the left, Bertha Mitchell, aged fourteen. (Chris Quick)

Hayle's first male voice choir in 1924, here pictured at Trevassick Farm. From left to right, back row: Willy Nicholas, Cyril Coombe, Kenneth Dunn, Willy Couch, Newell Matthews, John Quick. Middle row: Garfield Whear, Donald Whear, Bennett Williams, Freddy Harris, Reggie Dunn, Freddy Rutter. Front row: Kenneth Matthews, Herbert Matthews, Grandfather Pearce, Mrs Lello (his daughter), Joyce Quick, Bertha Quick, Edwin Lello. (Chris Quick)

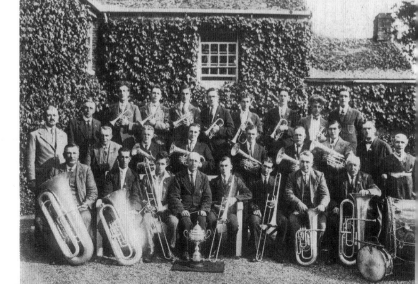

Hayle Town Band in the grounds of Penpol House, 1922. (Virginia Bliss)

HARBOUR

The 4,800-ton cruiser HMS *Bristol* being towed into Hayle Harbour to be scrapped in 1921. (Brian Sullivan)

The cruiser HMS *Bristol* alongside Carnsew Quay, waiting to be scrapped by Thomas Ward & Co. at the height of the ship breaking industry. She was one of a group of Navy vessels scrapped at Hayle in 1921. (Ronnie Williams Collection)

Fishing boats moored on the Steam Packet slipway. Hayle's only quayside hostelry, the Steam Packet Inn, was sited on the Bristolman's Dock on North Quay from 1811-1961, when it was demolished. The villas of Clifton Terrace stand on the cliff top behind the inn. (Chris Quick)

Boats moored on East Quay. The windlass post on the end of the Cockle Bank is still standing from the days of sailing ships, when it was used to turn them when leaving harbour. This quay was built by the Cornish Copper Co. on the entrance to South Quay, which at the time was the only quay owned by Harvey's. But due to a mistake in the location of the parish boundaries between Phillack and St Erth, it was proved to have been built on Harvey's land and the Copper Co. had to hand it over to their bitter enemies. (Chris Quick)

Dockers unloading on South Quay during the 1930s, possibly sugar beet. (Chris Quick)

The coal boat *Jubilence* aground at the entrance to Hayle Harbour in the 1970s. This situation happened on many occasions as the entrance to Hayle Harbour is difficult to navigate. (Hayle Archive)

The Graving Dock sluice gates, pictured in 1972. The dock was infilled in 1984, but is due to be restored in the current planned harbour regeneration scheme. (Ronnie Williams Collection)

The arches of Black Houses sluice at Carnsew Pool. The Hayle Canoe Club used the sluice for white-water training. (Andrew Szmidla)

EVENTS

Regatta Day in the 1920s. Hayle Regatta was a huge event held on August Bank Holiday, together with the carnival and a grand dance in the evening. Hundreds of spectators enjoyed a grand day out. (Hayle Archive)

Sailing dinghies waiting to take part in a Hayle Regatta during the 1930s. Competition was keen and sometimes resulted in mischievous pranks being played on fellow competitors to put them off their stride and lose the race. (Hayle Archive)

Spectators being rowed out on Copperhouse Pool, during the 1910 regatta. The row of cottages below Clifton Terrace was demolished in the 1950s. (Hayle Archive)

The Gipsies and the Dancing Bear. This unusual photograph of a group of people in carnival costumes was taken inside Bigglestone's shop in the early 1900s. (Hayle Archive)

Two magnificent carnival floats by J. & F. Pools entered in the 1948 procession. (Virginia Bliss)

Her Majesty the Queen passing through Hayle on her way from Geevor Mine at Pendeen to the Camborne School of Mines, 28 November 1980. (Ronnie Williams Collection)

RESCUE

Hayle's first lifeboat *Isis* being launched from the beach. She had no slipway and had to be pulled by horse-drawn trailer and launched into the surf. *Isis* was given to Hayle by the members of Oxford Union in 1866 and saved fifty-one lives during her twenty-one years of service. (Virginia Bliss)

Hayle's second lifeboat, *F.J. Harrison*, going to the aid of the *Escurial* wrecked off the coast at Portreath. Only two of the crew were saved from the wreck, eighteen seamen were drowned. (Hayle Archive)

The arrival of Hayle's third and last lifeboat, *Admiral Rodd*, in 1906. She was paraded with the town band through Foundry Square. The ladies on the right of the picture are holding RNLI collecting boxes. She served until 1920 when the Hayle Lifeboat Station was officially closed. (Malcolm Williams)

Godrevy Lighthouse and the rugged foreshore. As can be seen, the waters here need to be treated with great respect. This is also the location of the St Ives lifeboat *John and Sarah Eliza Stych* disaster in January 1939. Only one member of the crew survived. (Chris Quick)

ABOUT ST IVES TRUST ARCHIVE STUDY CENTRE

St Ives has, for over 600 years, been dependent on the fishing and mining industries and more recently on tourism and artists. Since 1996, the St Ives Trust Archive Study Centre, which is a charitable organisation run by about forty helpful and knowledgeable volunteers, has been assembling information on every aspect of the town and surrounding area. Its large and growing collection of newspaper articles, maps, legal documents, correspondence, catalogues and books, and its extensive collection of nearly 20,000 photographs, taken over the past 150 years, is always available to be viewed by the general public. The Centre also produces its own publications on different aspects of the town and its history. The Centre is a community archive and has close links with the local council, the local schools, churches, galleries and most of the organisations in the town. The Centre is open Tuesdays to Fridays from 10.00 a.m. until 4.00 p.m.

PREVIOUS PUBLICATIONS INCLUDE:

Janet Axten, *Gasworks to Gallery: The Story of Tate St Ives*, Axten and Orchard, 1995.

Peter Barnes, *Alfred Wallis & His Family: Fact and Fiction*, St Ives Trust Archive Study Centre, 1997.

Peter Murrish, *Prisoners of our Age: an account of the Second World War and its aftermath as it affected a small Cornish seaside town and a young Cornish Boy*, St Ives Trust Archive Study Centre, 1997.

Reprint of *A History of the Parishes of Saint Ives, Lelant, Towednack and Zennor in the County of Cornwall* by John Hobson Matthews, 1892, with additional material, St Ives Trust and St Ives Library, 2003.

Reprint of *Martin Cock's Guide to Saint Ives* by John Hobson Matthews, 1909, with additional material, St Ives Trust and St Ives Library, 2004.

Ted Lever and Nigel Jeyes, *Memories of Wartime St Ives*, St Ives Trust Archive Study Centre, 2005.

John McWilliams, *Maritime St Ives*, St Ives Trust Archive Study Centre, 2006.

John McWilliams, *A Century of Friendship: Breton Fishermen in Cornwall and Scilly* St Ives Trust, 2007.

Mary Quick, *Changing Times in Old St Ives* Volume 1, St Ives Trust Archive Study Centre, 2007.

Mary Quick, *Changing Times in Old St Ives* Volume 2, St Ives Trust Archive Study Centre, 2008.

Mary Quick, *Changing Times in Old St Ives* Volume 3, St Ives Trust Archive Study Centre, 2008.

Mary Quick, *Changing Times in Old St Ives* Volume 4, St Ives Trust Archive Study Centre, 2009.

CONTACT DETAILS:

St Ives Trust Archive Study Centre
Upper Parish Room
St Andrew's Street
St Ives
TR26 1AH
UK

Tel: 01736 796408   Email: archive@stivestrust.co.uk   Website: www.stivestrust.co.uk

The St Ives team. From left to right, back row: Mike Murphy, Rita Lait, Greta Williams, John Sell. Front row: Belinda Ratnayake, John McWilliams, Janet Axten, Lynn Burchess, Erica Sutcliffe, Karen Curnow.

ABOUT HAYLE COMMUNITY ARCHIVE

Hayle Community Archive was re-established in 2009 and is run on a volunteer basis. The Archive is operated from The Brewery Office which is the site of the old Ellis Brewery and was in operation in Hayle from the early 1800s until 1934. The old Brewery Office is a Grade II listed building which has been renovated and kindly let to the Archive group by Paul Stephens, who is the great grandson of Christopher Ellis, the last owner of the brewery.

The aim of the Hayle Community Archive is to collate archive material that relates to Hayle, and its surrounding areas, in one user-friendly space, allowing the material to be viewed by the public, and becoming the centre of excellence for the history of Hayle.

CONTACT DETAILS:

The Brewery Office
Sea Lane
Hayle
Cornwall
TR27 4DU
UK

Tel: 01736 753962   Email: email@haylearchive.org.uk   Website: www.haylearchive.org.uk

The Hayle team. From left to right: John Farrar, Pat Millett, Chris Quick, Georgina Schofield.

Other titles published by The History Press

Haunted St Ives
IAN ADDICOAT

St Ives has long been associated with strange hauntings. From heart-stopping account
apparitions, manifestations and related supernatural phenomena to first-hand encount
with ghouls and spirits, this collection contains new and well-known spooky stories
from around the town. Anyone interested in the supernatural history of this area will
fascinated in this phenomenal gathering of ghostly goings-on.

978 0 7524 4542 7

Fishing Boats of Cornwall
MIKE SMYLIE

The first deep-sea fishing boats of Cornwall are regarded as being influenced by the
three-masted French luggers that sailed over to cause havoc amongst the locals. How
fishing had been practised by Cornishmen for many generations before that, with
mackerel and pilchard fishing being prominent. After motorisation, the shape of the b
changed forever and the adaptation of old boats to accommodate engines is examine
are the famous yards and boatbuilders of Cornwall still operational today.

978 0 7524 4906 7

Cornish Family Names
BOB RICHARDS

The Cornish have for a long time long considered themselves a race apart from the
English and their origins are indeed more related to those of the Welsh, Scottish and
Breton peoples than to most others east of the River Tamar. This handy lexicon, draw
together from an exhaustive research, serves as an ideal starting point for tracing ance
Packed with information about notable families and migration, this is also an ideal bc
for anyone interested in the story of Cornish people.

978 0 7524 4976 0

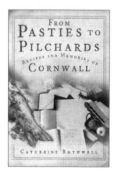

From Pasties to Pilchards: Memories and Recipes of Cornwa
CATHERINE ROTHWELL

Catherine Rothwell has gathered together over 130 traditional Cornish recipes in he
latest book. Cornwall has always had a strong culinary tradition, with many dishes
having their origins in the county. Interwoven with recipes are stories and anecdotes
from Catherine's contributors, as well as historical tales of the places featured, this is a
fascinating read not only for those interested in regional cookery, but also in local his
customs and traditions.

978 0 7524 4908 1

Visit our website and discover thousands of other History Press books.
www.thehistorypress.co.uk